Get in the Ark

Judy Johnson

GET IN THE ARK

ISBN: 978-1-60920-038-1

Library of Congress Cataloging-in-Publication Data

Unless otherwise indicated, all Scripture quotations are from the *New International Version* of the Bible.

All other references will be designated in the *Notes* section at the end or designated by abbreviation within the text as follows:

All Scriptures marked NAS are from the *New American Standard Bible.*

All Scriptures marked KJV are from the *King James Version.*

All Scriptures marked NKJ are from the *New King James.*

All Scriptures marked LB are from *The Living Bible.*

The author has included all parentheses, italics and bold-faced words for emphasis or explanation. Satan or devil are not capitalized, unless the first word of a sentence, so as not to give recognition to the archenemy. Other words, pertaining to Salvation, Heaven, God, attributes such as Mercy and Grace, His Church, or their pronouns, are capitalized contrary to the rules of grammar, in order to acknowledge their special importance to the message and the *things of God* that are being mentioned.

API
Ajoyin Publishing, Inc.
P.O. 342
Three Rivers, MI 49093

www.ajoyin.com

Please direct your inquiries to admin@ajoyin.com

CONTENTS

A New Day   1

Day 1   *Isaiah 42:9*   2

Day 2   *Isaiah 43:19 NLT*   4

Day 3   *Isaiah 43:19 NLT*   6

Day 4   *Romans 8:32 NKJ*   8

Day 5   *Amos 3:7 NKJ*   10

Day 6   *Genesis 7:4 NKJ*   12

Day 7   *I Corinthians 2:13 NIV*   14

Day 8   *Revelation 3:20 NKJ*   16

Day 9   *Joshua 3:15 & 16 NLT*   18

Day 10   *Joshua 3:8 NIV*   20

Day 11   *Isaiah 45:2 NLT*   22

Day 12   *Romans 6:4*   24

Day 13   *Genesis 7:1 NIV*   26

Day 14   *Psalm 127:1 NIV*   28

Day 15   *Ephesians 2:19*   30

Day 16   *I Corinthians 5:7 NKJ*   32

Day 17   *Ephesians 4:10*   34

Day 18   *Genesis 8:4 NIV*   36

Day 19   *Colossians 2:14*   38

Day 20   *Matthew 24:38 & 39*   40

Day 21   *Romans 5:12 NKJ*   42

Day 22   *Luke 11:26*   44

Day 23   *John 1:16*   46

Day 24   *Exodus 3:2 NKJ*   48

Day 25   *Matthew 14:29*   50

Day 26   *Exodus 2:3 NL*   52

Day 27   *Matthew 24:38 & 39*   54

Day 28   *Exodus 3:2 NKJ*   56

Day 29   *Malachi 4:5 & 6 KJV*   58

Day 30   *John 17:3 NKJ*   60

Day 31   *Hebrews 13:8*   62

His All Sufficiency   64

Notes   66

Addendum   68

Pray   70

A New Day

"There's nothing new
under the sun,
nothing new
that man's not done":

So, said Solomon
long ago,
as he saw his days
filled with woe.

But, God says—

"I do a New Thing!
I do something thought
never shall be.

In Isaiah,
chapter forty and three,
I do a New Thing:
look and see!

Never mind, what's
come to pass.
I do a New Thing
that'll, surely, last.

It's a work that I
long-ago planned,
a New Work sweeping
over this Land.

Open your eyes
and you will see;
you'll see the New Work
begun by Me.

There's nothing like it,
ever, before.
But, you must march
through the Open Door!

There's nothing like it
under the sun.
Open your eyes:
see what I've begun.

Come into your future
that's bright with glee!
Come march higher,
much higher with Me!

There's nothing like it
on the earth.
It's something I'm
about ready to birth.

Get ready, I say.
Get ready and see.
Get ready, to enter
the Vision with Me!"

Day 1

*Behold, the former things are come to pass, and new things do I **declare**: before they spring forth I **tell** you of them.*

The Changeless God of Order *and* The Ever Fresh God of Change

There are three things we need to take note of, in understanding the *will* and *purposes* of God:

- God is a God of **patterns**
- God is a God of **timing**, and
- God is a God of **levels**

God **operates by patterns,** according to set **times** and **seasons,** and moves from **level to level,** or put another way, in **cycles.**

God operates frequently, as such, in *recognizable patterns,* because He is a God of **order.** Nevertheless, God is *not always predictable,* for He is not a prisoner of His own order, or ways of operating, in the past.

As a *God of levels,* He is **constantly moving** us, from one level to the next. It is much like climbing a mountain or stairs. For, *God is on the move.* Like the river, He is **ever flowing.** Like the mighty wind, He is **ever blowing.**

As to His *character*, He is the **same,** yesterday, today, and forever.[1] As to His *methods of operation,* we can say, "God is doing a **New Thing!**" We say it, for **God has declared it!**

This *never-changing God,* as to His character, is **eternally fresh** in His *works* and *operations.* Therefore, He can do a *New Thing!*

Isaiah 42:9

I'm readying a Brand-New Thing!

See! I've, already, begun.
I'm making a pathway
through the wilderness
for My people to "Come."

I create Rivers for them
in the desert sun;
I make blinded eyes to see.

I make roads for them
in the wilderness;
I give them **New Songs to sing!**

Paths before them
are straightened
and darkened things
made light.

The blind, I bring
by **a new way,**
making all
crooked things right.

Day 2

*For I am about to do a brand-new thing. See, I have already begun! Do you see it? I will make a **pathway** through the wilderness for my people **to come home**. I will create **rivers** for them in the desert!*

IT IS REVIVAL TIME!

The Church is moving into a *new season*—it is a **new DAY**, a **new WAY**, and a **new CHURCH!**

The Church, made up of all who believe in Jesus Christ, as His corporate body, has been out in the desert, walking through a **hot, arid**, and **barren** wilderness.

"It is **time**," God says. "It is *time* for the Church to be **revived**." He wants to **refresh, renew,** and **restore** Her. Rivers, in the desert, are not the *usual*. But, God is about to do the *unusual*.

Father God wants to bring His Church **Home**. Therefore, He has created a *pathway* for Her to come. This pathway leads back to the **Father's House**.

To follow this path, back to the Father, means we must *leave* some old familiar paths and *forsake* some old ways of thinking. We are told in Isaiah 55:7-9:

> *"Let the wicked **forsake** his way, and the unrighteous man his thoughts: and let him **return** unto the Lord, and He will have mercy upon him; and to our God, for He will abundantly pardon. For My thoughts are not your thoughts, neither are your ways My ways, saith the Lord."*

4

Isaiah 43:19 NLT

We must arise and get out of the pits and valleys of **low-ways** of thinking, to which the Church has fallen, and begin to climb and transcend the heights and peaks of God's Glory.

As a man thinks in his heart, so is he.[1] We are *becoming* what we think, by being *conformed*, into the very thing we visualize of ourselves. For this reason, our minds must be **transformed**, to enable us to think God's thoughts, after Him.

Only as, we become **God-inside minded,** will we be able to climb new heights of revelation and leave the desert of "low thinking" below.

As the Church *glimpsed* **Christ's blood**—it was **redeemed!** Now, She must enter within the veil and, there, *glimpse* **His Glory,** that She may be **transformed!**[2]

I am doing a **NEW THING;**
I have, already, begun.

I am making a **PATHWAY,**
for My people to come:

A **PATH** in the wilderness,
I am bringing them **HOME!**

"**Come out** of that desert:
There, no more roam!"

Day 3

For I am about to do a brand-new thing. See I have already begun!
Do you see it? I will make a pathway through the wilderness for my
people to come home. I will create rivers for them in the desert.

HOUSE OF COVENANT

Father God wants to bring His Church Home. Therefore, He has
created a *pathway* for Her that leads to the *Father's House*—a
House of Covenant!

Covenant is not a subject, well, understood by the Church, today.
But, everything God does, in relationship to Israel and His Church,
is based upon it.

God, being a father, relates to His Church in terms of *fatherhood,*
sonship, and *family,* just, as He did with Israel. For, Heaven is the
Home of His **Eternal Family**.

This concept is very important to those growing up, *without* the
security and comforts of a home life, in a real family environment,
or *without* stable, loving parents, who care for them, especially, with
a dad, who is present in the home.

Like those, in this generation, I have experienced much pain and
sorrow. In times of the greatest difficulty and discouragement, God
has asked me, personally, **"Have I brought you this far to leave you?"**
Those words brought much comfort and courage to go on.

As I considered those words and counted the cost of God's bringing me to the place, where I was at that time, then, I realized Father
God was saying, **"I have paid, too, dear a price for you, to forsake**
you, now. I intend to see you through, to the end."[1]

Isaiah 43:19 NLT

God sent His Son
I cannot deny;
To prove His love,
for me He died.

Why would He, then,
turn His back
and, now, from me
His love retract?

This dreadful fear
is a total lie
the devil wants
you and me to buy.

If he can make us pout,
be full of fear and to doubt,
then, we will live
as Israel did,

Who, in the wilderness,
cried and pled,
thinking God so unfair:

A fickle God, who would
abandon them, there!

Day 4

*He who did **not spare His own Son**, but **delivered Him up** for us all,
how shall He not **with Him** also freely give us all things?*

Abandon Imprisoned Thinking

Israel was troubled in the Wilderness, with *fear* of being **forsaken**
and **abandoned, in their time of need.** Perhaps, this *faulty percep-
tion* of God began in the 400 years of bondage and tyranny, under
Egyptian rule. Their **orphaned** and **imprisoned thinking,** engrained
in them by their taskmasters, never, seemingly, left them, even, after
being delivered.

"Have I brought you out here to leave you?" This was a question
deserving of Israel's consideration. Why would God call Abraham,
give him a miracle-child, a vision of national blessings, then, over-
see Jacob through his long pilgrimage, Joseph through his afflic-
tions in an Egyptian prison, preserve the nation for 400 years of
bondage, to, finally, raise up a deliverer, trained in Egypt, prepared
in the wilderness, that He might lead His people out, **if He were,
only, planning to abandon them, there?**

Stop, to consider all the events, involved in the fulfillment of, just,
one of God's prophetic promises! How can we, honestly, doubt His
sovereign *involvement?* **God will do what He says He will do!**

Just, to *bring Israel out of Egypt* required the visitation of ten
plagues upon the land, people, and gods of Egypt. Over a million
people crossed the Red Sea on dry land, in the middle of the night,
wherein Pharaoh and his army drowned. God, then, *led, protected*
and *provided* for this multitude, *daily,* over the next forty years.

Romans 8:32 NKJ

Yet, despite, such, insurmountable evidence, confirming the love and intervention of Almighty God, some, still, fretted and protested, that He brought them out in the wilderness—ONLY, TO DESTROY THEM![1]

Does this make sense? Hear God's words: **"Have I brought you this far to forsake you?"** Neither has He brought you this far to forsake you, either. **Don't you forsake Him!**

Consider what it has cost God, just, to bring you, to where you are, right now. What He is doing, in your life, is no less a feat and miracle, than it was in the Nation Israel. If He spared not His, only, Son **for you**—He will, *with Him*, also, freely give you **all things!**

> Of God's involvement,
> I cannot doubt.
> I must not fret;
> I must not pout.
>
> Just, as He delivered Israel
> and brought them out,
> God knows what He's a'doing
> and what He's about!

Day 5

*Surely the Lord God does nothing, unless He **reveals** His secrets to His servants the **prophets**.*

It is Time!

By the **Lord's Word,** Noah knew seven days were **determined,** before the rains would *come*; and forty days and forty nights were **determined,** for the rains to *continue*.

Had God not **informed** Noah, of such, there could have been room for alarm in Noah and his family, as night after night and day after day, the stormy rains continued.

However, God chooses to do nothing, without, first, telling His prophets. He is a precise God, doing nothing willy-nilly. Even, in time of darkness or uncertainty, He has **had a plan** and **revealed that plan** to His prophets.

God told Jeremiah, there would be 70 years of captivity, for the people of God, and, then, deliverance would come. God **revealed,** unto His **prophet** Jeremiah, the **set time** for the *fulfillment* of His **decree.**

"God's Word" to His prophets is, so, reliable that Daniel read the decree that the prophet Jeremiah recorded, concerning the captivity and the timeline for their release, while he was in captivity. Therefore, Daniel began *interceding*. He reminded God, **"It is time!"** Then, having repented for his nation, Daniel called for the **fulfillment** of "God's Word" **decreed,** on behalf of His people.

Meanwhile, God was stirring the heart of the new king, Cyrus of Persia, to fulfill the "Word of the LORD," as given Jeremiah. There-

Amos 3:7 NKJ

fore, a proclamation was made, to allow the return of the people from captivity, to rebuild and **restore worship to the city of Jerusalem.**

God is **restoring another city,** today. He is restoring worship in **Zion, the City of God,** in a remnant of believers, called the Church. The prophets, who hear God's Voice and obey His Word, are once, again, saying: **"It is time!"**

Lord, it is time,
as Your prophets say.
We are, now, in
a Brand-New Day.

You are restoring
Your City, again.
It is time for a
New Work to begin.

Like Daniel of old,
may we *intercede*
and call on the Word,
You have *decreed.*

Restore Your Bride.
Raise up Her walls,
of generations past,
till Your Remnant stands tall!

Day 6

*For **after seven more days** I will cause it to rain on the earth forty days
and forty nights, and I will destroy from the face of the earth all living
things that I have made.*

Rest-Waiting

It was important for Noah to **hear God,** because there were **seven
days of, just, waiting,** in a sealed ark full of animals, before the rains,
finally, began.

Had Noah not known, through God's instruction, that this would
be His plan, he and all aboard might have become *alarmed* and
fearful, when the rains did not fall, immediately. Noah might have
spent this *waiting-time,* instead, trying to comfort and assure those
aboard that these strange circumstances did not mean they had
missed God, as they questioned.

They might, also, have found occasion to exit the ark, as those
outside shouted ridicules and insults, when the rains did not come,
as predicted. I can hear those outside, pounding at the door in
mockery and revelry, causing the animals to move about, nervously.

But, because, *by the Word of the LORD,* **Noah knew there were seven
days determined** and, then, the rains would come, and **forty days
and forty nights were determined** for the rains to fall, Noah and
his family had only, therefore, to *rest in His Word* and *rest in His
Love.*

Genesis 7:4 NKJ

I, too, can **rest**
in God's Love and Word,
because, like Noah,
His Word I've **heard**.

I'm assured, as I
rely upon this Word,
in God's **timing,**
His will, I'll give birth!

What God says
will **come to pass.**
Though earth perish,
His Word will last.

When others doubt,
and mockingly spout,
I'll, still, believe I'll see
God's Word come about!

I'll believe what God has decreed:
a sure word, a promised seed.

Cause, His promises cannot fail:
Against God's Church,
evil will not prevail!

Day 7

This is what we speak, not in words taught us by human wisdom but in words taught by the Spirit, expressing spiritual truths in spiritual words.

Enter the Vision with Me

The Father's invitation and request to His Church is, "Enter the things I have **prepared** for you."

> *"No eye has seen, nor ear has heard, nor mind has conceived what God has **prepared** for those who love him."[1]*

"But God has **revealed** it to us by His Spirit."[2] Therefore, we must get into the Spirit realm to see them. John said, in Revelation 1:10,

> *"On the Lord's Day I was **in the Spirit**, and I heard behind me a loud voice like a trumpet."*

A little bit later, God, also, spoke to John, as he saw a door **open** in Heaven:

> *"'**Come up here**, and I will show you what must happen after these things.' And instantly I was in the Spirit"[3]*

We have entered into the Third Day, the Day of the LORD. If we are to see the LORD in His Glory, we must get in the Spirit. We must be brought to the level of His thoughts and ways.[4] Beholding His Glory, we will, then, be **changed** into that same image, from Glory to Glory.

I Corinthians 2:13 NIV

We need God's image for us. What we envision is what we'll *become.* Therefore, we must envision what God has **prepared for us,** so we may **enter** that vision.

As Christ *was* on this earth, so His Church *is to be,* now.[5] By being **in agreement** with the Spirit, in all our *thoughts* and *ways,* the Spirit-Life will be in operation in our actions, as well. Then, as we *think,* **so we will be;** as Christ was on earth, **so we will become!**

The Father has sent out the invitation, bidding those who will, **"Come."** He is calling those, previously, considered *poor, crippled, blind,* and *lame,* **"Come!"**[6]

> **Come!** The Master calls,
> **Come** and dine.
> You are welcome all the time.
>
> At My table, place your feet,
> where, in fellowship,
> we shall meet!
>
> **Enter the things**
> **prepared** by Me;
> for, this is your year
> of Jubilee!

Day 8

*Behold, I stand at the door and knock. If anyone **hears** My Voice and **opens the door**, I will come in to him and dine with him, and he with Me.*

THE OPEN DOOR

When the Church **opens its door** to the LORD, the **LORD opens His Door** to higher things.[1]

A **Door of opportunity** has **opened** before the Church. Like John, Jesus is calling us *upward*: "**Come up Higher.**"

Come up higher in the Spirit. You must be in the Spirit, on the LORD'S DAY, to see into the realm of the Spirit. Only, then, can you *perceive* what God is doing on earth. Only, then, can you *discern* the **times** and **seasons** of the LORD. Only, then, can you perceive that, which He has *predetermined* for you.

Noah heard the LORD say, "Noah, **come into the ark**, you and all your household."[2] Noah stepped through the **open door** of the ark, before him, into his *future* and *destiny*. Noah obeyed the Voice of the LORD.

Noah and his family "went into the ark, because of the coming waters of the flood."[3] They did so *by faith*, because they had not witnessed the floodwaters, as yet. They had, only, **heard** the Word of the LORD:

> *"For after seven more days I will cause it to rain on the earth forty days and forty nights."*[4]

Revelation 3:20 NKJ

Now, it was important that Noah *heard* and *received* this Word, from the LORD. For, after Noah, the family, and all the appointed animals were aboard, God **shut the door!**[5] And, **sealed it!** Nobody, else, was allowed aboard, once the door was closed.

There are **doors of opportunity** God gives us, in His **appointed times** and **purposes.** If we refuse to *hear* and *heed*, we could find ourselves left on the shores of our destiny, shut out, only, to await the fearful judgments of God.

Time is wasting:
Don't slack!
Heed God's message:
Get on track!

The Great Move of God
is about to begin.
There's **no time,** now,
for living in sin!

You're liable **to miss**
your **appointed time,**
if, your *place* in the kingdom,
you don't *find!*

Day 9

*Now it was **the harvest season**, and the Jordan was **overflowing its banks**. But as soon as the feet of the priests who were carrying the Ark touched the water **at the river's edge**, the water began piling up at a town upstream called Adam.*

Doorway to a Move of God

It is at the **brink** that one comes to the **threshold** where *time* and *destiny* meet, for a *divine encounter*. At the **brink**, an opportunity presents itself, to step into a **new level** and climb to a **new height** in God.

The **brink of the river** was, often, the **doorway** into that, which was *new*, that which was *greater*, that which was *God!*

- **At the brink of the river**, Moses held out his rod and a multitude *crossed over*, on their way to a *New Land*.

- **At the brink of the river**, a vision of God presented itself to an Egyptian Pharaoh, which, when interpreted by Joseph, became the **doorway** for the preservation of a *Nation*.

- **At the brink of the river**, as the priesthood of God stepped into the floodwaters, the **pathway opened** unto the promises of God, for a people of God, who followed the priests of God—to a *Land* of *Promise*.

- **At the brink of the flood**, yet to come, Noah *stepped across the door*, at God's command, into a *New World*, a *New Time!*

- At the brink of the waters of a tumultuous sea, Peter *stepped out of his boat of mediocrity* into a **supernatural walk**, buoyed on the wings of faith.

Joshua 3:15 & 16 NLT

At the brink of the river, one will meet the *greatest obstacles to faith*.

At the brink of the river, one will meet the *greatest opportunity to fail*. One cannot look back and succeed. One cannot go back and proceed.

It is **at the brink of the river** one advances into the **new,** the **now,** the **next** move of God.

You have **come to the River's brink.**
You will not fail;
You will not sink.

This is **a place I have ordained.**
So, step right in
and, so, obtain.

Enter in your Promised Land.
be enlarged
and, there, expand!

Day 10

*Tell the priests who carry the Ark of the Covenant: When you reach the **edge** of the Jordan's waters, go and **stand in the river**.*

AT THE THRESHOLD!

The Church is at the threshold of something BIG! Just, as Moses, who stood at the **threshold,** or **door,** of the crossing of the Red Sea. As he held out the Rod of God in his hand, the waters *broke* and the river *opened!*

As we are come to the **New Door,** at the **threshold,** it is the LORD that *opens* or enables us to *crossover.* Just, as the enemy, led by Pharaoh, drowned at that crossing, so, the LORD will destroy the enemy that would try to prevent ours.

The Church is standing at the **threshold of Her opportunity.** She has been lying, impotent, unable to reach the *moving of the waters* at the *proper time* and *season.* Jesus is passing by! He is asking her, "Will you let Me make you whole?" Those who have hindered Her in the past are, now, not able, because the **Breaker** is *there.*

A certain man was *there,* at the pool of Bethesda, when Jesus passed by, just, as the Church is *there,* now, in the *right place,* in the *right hour* of the *moving of the waters.* Hear Jesus say to Her, as He said to the man: "Arise!"

Jesus is asking His Church, "Will you allow Me to **change You?**" The River is, often, contrary to the opinion and methods of denominational and traditional channels. Therefore, He is asking His Church, "Will you allow Me to **create new channels** in You?" *This requires change.*

Joshua 3:8 NIV

Jesus asked permission of the man, at the pool, to **restore** him to *usefulness* and *freedom*. He is asking His Church, to allow Him to *renovate* and *make changes* in Her, that will bring Her to the **fulfillment of Her destiny**, or She must be left behind.

The Spirit of Prophesy is saying: **"Get Up! Stand** Up! **Mount** Up! **Climb** Up! **Soar** Upward, Church! "This is Your **hour** of destiny.

Jesus is come!
Time has begun,
for changes to come
and God's will to be done.

Church arise!
Mount up to the skies.
Daily sacrifice,
to gain the prize.

Harvest is ripe!
Rush to the plight
of those in the night,
wielding Your light!

Day 11

I will smash down gates of bronze and cut through bars of iron. And I will give you the treasures hidden in the darkness—secret riches.

THE BREAKER!

The **Breaker** goes before, so we can **breakout** into a *wealthy place.* He breaks us out into the *open*, into a place of *increase*, from a place of *confinement.*

Whenever we *breakout*, **new things** are made available to us, in order that we can go forth, into **new places**, in **new territory**. To go to *new territory*, we must be willing to go to the **Brink!**

The **Brink** is the *threshold*, to something *new* and something *big!* It is *at the threshold*, we **crossover**. And, it is *at the threshold* we will **meet our adversary.**

Therefore, the **Brink**, or the *threshold*, is the place of *greatest risk.* It is, also, the place of *greatest potential* and *opportunity*. It represents an **Open Door.**

We must go to the **Brink** or *edge* and *risk l*oosing all, in order to *pass through* and *possess,* what lies **on the other side.** Therefore, we must, successfully, face the *obstacles at the threshold.*

The enemies of our destiny are not the, only, ones guarding the threshold. There is another. His name is **Breaker.** He, it is, who will **break us through** the enemy line, into our *future*, into the *new*, into the *now* of God.

Isaiah 45:2 NLT

As tradition goes, when a groom marries, he, then, must carry his newly wed *over the threshold* of their new home. **Jesus,** the **Breaker,** as our **Bridegroom,** will carry His Bride *across the threshold* of Her *future,* as well.

As we **cross the threshold,** He is bringing us into a place of *renewed freedom.* There, He will release us, into a *new* and *greater realm,* of His purpose and power.

The **Brink** or *threshold,* therefore, becomes the **doorway** for His Church, to **enter** into the **Glory of God!**

Jesus my Breaker
is breaking a Way,
advancing His Bride
into Her brand New Day!

Lo, I set before you
an **Open Door!**
Fear not to enter.
Just, do what you're told!

Then, I will defeat
every adversary, there,
as I **carry My Bride,**
to the place, we shall share!

Day 12

*Therefore we are buried with Him by baptism into death: that like as Christ was **raised up** from the dead by the glory of the Father, even so we also should **walk in newness of life**.*

Noah's New Day!

When Noah *went through* the **open door** of the ark, he was **stepping into** a **new day** and a **new way,** in a **new era** of a **new world.**

As the waters rose, the ark was *lifted heavenward,* to a **new destination,** coming to rest on a mountaintop, *high above* all that lay below.[1]

Noah *emerged* from this ark **not the same man.** He *entered,* a citizen of one world, to *exit* a citizen of another. This very truth pictures for us what happens, when one is **born-again** or **born-from-above.**[2]

According to 1 Corinthians 5:17, when we are b*orn-again, into Christ,* we become **new creations** of God. The old is passed away and **all things become new.**

Noah, *stepping into the ark,* pictured us *stepping into Jesus,* our Salvation, *leaving* the past and *entering* into something entirely new, which has never been. His relationship to the old world was, now, gone. The old world, having died to him and he to it, Noah, then, pictured being **raised to newness of life,** within the Ark, as we are raised to **newness of life, in Christ Jesus.**

Romans 6:4

I'll step through the Door
to my Promised Land,
where I can grow,
where I can expand.

My borders I'll span
to a higher dimension,
as I lengthen my stakes,
to reach my vision.

I'll move on forward;
I'll climb a little higher,
ever moving
ever aspiring.

I'll reach for the goal
set for me
by Father God,
beyond Crystal Sea.

I'll keep on moving
up that mountain,
going round and round,
cycle after cycle.

I'll revolve,
until, safely, I arrive
in His likeness,
to, contently, abide!

Day 13

The LORD then said to Noah, "Go into the ark, you and your whole family, because I have found you righteous in this generation.

GET IN THE ARK!

We have been coming and appearing before the Ark, daily, building and working. Suddenly, the Father says, **"Get in the Ark!** Get in *that,* which you've *been building."*

If we had known that what we've been building, must, now, *keep us afloat,* would we have *built any differently?* Would we have used *different materials?*

But, alas, if we've been following instructions and building, only, as God has directed, shouldn't that which we've constructed, now, prove **sea-worthy?** Shouldn't we be ready and prepared, for what is coming?

God knows when our work on one level is done and we are ready for the next. He knows when our *preparation time* is complete. When it is, He must move us on, to the next phase—we must **proceed through the Open Door,** to the **next move of God!**

Father God, like Noah, is telling His Family—**GET IN THE ARK!**

GENESIS 7:1 NIV

You've been building
you know not what.
I have been watching,
after what you've **sought**.

Has it been Me,
you desire most to see?
Mercy drops are falling:
I'm what you need!

Get in the Ark!
I am the ONE:
the one you've been seeking:
God's, very, own Son.

If you do not **know Me,**
in the work
you have done,
it is, then,
not the work,
the work of the Son.

Night is, now, falling.
Soon, all work must be done:

Get in the Ark, Jesus—
afore judgment's begun!

Day 14

*Unless **the LORD builds the house,** they labor in vain who **build it;** unless the LORD guards the city, the watchman stays awake in vain.*

The Ark God Built

Father God is telling His Family—"Get in the Ark!" He **provided this** Ark for His Household, just, as father **Noah provided the ark,** that sanctuaried his own family, from the flood.

Father God became the **pattern,** to His own *plan.* True to type, He **built the ark,** for the *preservation* of the Family of God, to the *saving* of His Household.

And, when the work was **complete**—He told His Family: "It is **FINISHED!"**[1] Therefore, "Get in!" The **finished work** of Christ is the *provision* of the Father, for the *protection* and *preservation* of the Family of God.

Our Ark, Jesus, is **watertight** and **sea-worthy.** He is *sufficiently, able* to *uphold* and *bear* every living thing that comes aboard.[2] By Him, all things *exist, consist,* and are *held together!*[3]

This **ship will survive** every storm of life. He proved *sea-worthy,* by first *surviving* everything the world and the devil could throw at Him, for 33 years. Therefore, we can rest assured, that He is *able to sustain us,* through all our storms of life. **We, too, will survive** them all, if we *abide* in Him.

PSALM 127:1 NIV

Behold, how the world
has labored and fraught,
while knowing not Me
nor, after Me sought.

All their work
must, now, come to naught,
for, while they labored,
Me, they forgot!

◻   ◻   ◻

There is, only, **one Ship**
that shall weather
the seas.

That Ship was **provided**
for you and for me.

I, therefore, will not build
what Father has not!

I will get in the Ship
that Father has bought
with His own Son
on Calvary's Tree:

**A Ship that can weather
every storm and rough sea!**

Day 15

*Now therefore ye are no more strangers and foreigners, but fellow citizens with the saints, and of the **household of God**.*

HOUSEHOLD SALVATION!

God brought **Noah and his family** into the ark and, thereby, saved both he and his **household**. Once inside, God shut the door, *securing* them.

Noah had followed God's instruction to *pitch* the ark **without** and **within** with a **watertight pitch**, *sealing* it from the floods, that would, soon, beat upon it. They were sheltered *within*, from the death and judgment that, soon, would fall *without*.

In Egypt, God instructed Israel to assemble, *inside* their *dwelling place*, behind closed door, **covered and marked by the blood** of a sacrificial lamb. When the death angel, bringing judgment, passed that way, they would be *spared*.

The Israelites were *safe* and *secure*, as each father obeyed and prepared a lamb, to **cover his family**. The death angel could not penetrate that bloody barrier that *sealed the door* of their home.

Death came to the door of those *not covered by blood* and entered in, to take their firstborn. Allegiance to the Egyptian system and its gods brought death and destruction. To embrace their idols and remain loyal to them *meant certain judgment and death*, to the firstborn.

There was a firstborn that was sacrificed, in place of the firstborn that should have died. The death, of God's firstborn Son, means *safety* to all behind the **blood of the Lamb**, whose blood the Father has placed **on the doorposts** for **His Household**, the Family of God.

Ephesians 2:19

We are *safe* and *secure,* when we *take shelter* in the provision of the Lamb, and, thus, **abide in the Father's House.**

Come inside
and hide;
abide,
to survive,
alive.

The Lamb died,
was sacrificed,
shed His blood,
your sins
to hide.

The Father gave,
from hell
to save,
and rescue from
a fiery grave,

—**all, who in His
Household, stay!**

Day 16

*Therefore purge out the old leaven, that you may be a new lump, since you truly are unleavened. For indeed **Christ, our Passover**, was sacrificed for us.*

OUR PASSOVER SLAIN

The "seventeenth day" of the seventh month represents the **end of the ordeal,** dealing or judgment of God that ends in **victory,** for the believer.[1] Another, date, as equally, important and preceding it, is the "fourteenth day" of the month, representing **salvation** or **deliverance.**[2]

On the **fourteenth** of the month, the children of Israel were **delivered** from Egyptian bondage. Three days later, they passed through the Red Sea, picturing **resurrection.** As they stepped onto the other side, dry and safe, they sang:[3]

> *"The LORD is my strength and my song; He has become my salvation."*

True to the **pattern,** this "fourteenth day" appears, again, in history, in unison with events that are tied to the "seventeenth day". The **Passover** celebration occurred on that fourteenth day.[4]

Our Lord Jesus *began* the fourteenth day, **eating the Passover** with His disciples. He *ended* the fourteenth day **slain, as the Passover Lamb.** This is because Jewish time is reckoned, from one evening to the next.

I Corinthians 5:7 NKJ

Jesus, then, spent three days and nights, from the fourteenth to the seventeenth, in the heart of the earth, to *resurrect* on the *third*. *Three* added to *fourteen* becomes seventeen, the **end of the ordeal,** which again reflects *triumph, victory* over sin and death, and *resurrection.*

Fourteen stands for *deliverance* or *salvation.* Our personal deliverance and salvation takes place, when we come **under the blood of Christ, our Passover!**[5]

Jesus our Passover
for us sacrificed,
was resurrected, as pictured
by events mentioned **thrice:**

Once, in the flood
to walk on dry land.
Once, in triumph,
the Red Sea to expand.

Again, in triumph,
on Resurrection Day,
when an empty tomb witnessed
where Jesus had lain.

How significant:
the meaning
that's hidden in **three,**
picturing resurrection,
the power that sets free!

Day 17

He that descended is the same also that ascended up far above all heavens, that He might fill all things.

WINNOWED: AT THE THRESHING FLOOR

Ruth received an *earnest* and the *promise* of the **fullness** of her *inheritance,* while waiting **at the threshing floor** of Boaz. At the *threshing floor,* **separation** takes place, of the husk from the grain.

The three great events that correspond to the 17th day of the 7th month, are pictures of **three great threshing floors,** where:

1. At the **flood**—a *family* is *separated* unto God, from all the families of the earth.

2. At the **Red Sea**—a *nation* is *separated* unto God, from all the nations of the earth.

3. At the **Cross**—provision is made for a **world** to be *separated* unto God.

Just, as God met Gideon, at the *threshing floor* of Ophrah, and met David, at the *threshing floor* of Ornan, God will, yet, meet His Remnant Church at **His threshing floor.**

Like Ruth met Boaz, the LORD is desirous for His Bride to come to **His threshing floor,** where He can bring Her into **fullness.** But, the Church must, first, be willing to, there, be *separated, fully, unto Him.* Therefore, His instructions are:

EPHESIANS 4:10

*I will dwell in them, and walk in them; and I will be their God,
and they shall be My People. 'Wherefore come out from among
them, and be ye separate, saith the LORD, and touch not the
unclean thing; and I will receive you.'*[1]

Jesus, eagerly, awaits His Bride's **appearance at the threshing floor**
and their **becoming one,** so She may come *into Her inheritance* and
receive of His fullness.

*For the earnest expectation of the creation eagerly waits
for the **revealing** of the Sons of God.*[2]

Threshing *isn't an easy thing,*
as He **separates, winnows,**
and in the air flings.

Yet, it is a necessary one,
if I would with Him,
from yon, Throne above,
jointly rule, both He and I:

I the one, for whom He died;
He the one, who sacrificed;
that I may with Him, there, abide,
jointly ruling, by His side—

as Husbandman and His Bride!

Day 18

And on the seventeenth day of the seventh month the ark came to rest on the mountains of Ararat.

THE EVENTFUL SEVENTEENTH DAY

The *"end of the 'ordeal'"* is represented by the **seventeenth day of the seventh month.** This, very, important date is the first of three, such, occurrences in Scripture. The, first, two are types or shadows, of the major event, that occurred on the third.

The number *seventeen* is, very, significant in Scripture, as the *seventh prime* or indivisible number. Its primary meaning is **Victory.**[1]

Seventeen is, also, a compound of the numbers *seven* and *ten. Seven* signifies **completeness,** while *ten* signifies **testimony.** Combined, *seventeen* represents **the testimony of completeness or victory found in Christ Jesus.**[2]

Therefore, these 3 occurrences of the date, the *seventeenth day of the seventh month*, bear significance in revealing the **complete victory that is in Christ Jesus.** To what do these 3 occurrences refer?

- the **Flood**
- the Crossing of the **Red Sea,** and
- the Crucifixion of Christ on the **Cross**

The **Flood** is the first, of three important events in Scripture that preaches **"the Gospel,"** or **"the Complete Work of Christ on the Cross,"** for mankind's Salvation.

GENESIS 8:4 NIV

Because the focus of these three events has, primarily, been one of judgment upon sin, wickedness, or the wicked, we have, often, missed its parallel truth: *their significance,* as they *relate to the believer.*

Come and see, what I have done
and, yet, surely, I've only begun:

The horse and the rider,
thrown into the Sea;

My Son, dying on Calvary;

All mankind, drowned in a flood,
lifting Noah and family, above!

All, these happened
that I might show:
My Covenant Love,
seen in My Bow:

A rainbow painted
in the sky,
to remind mankind:

**My Love, I cannot,
I shall not deny!**

Day 19

*Blotting out the handwriting of ordinances that was against us, which was contrary to us, and **took it out of the way, nailing it to the cross.***

PAID IN FULL

The Greek word *teletestai,* meaning *"it is finished",* was written across every certificate of debt, when **paid in full.** The certificate was, then, nailed to the doorpost of the debtor's house, displaying within sight of all the public, that this debt was **finished.**

Jesus is the Door of Salvation. His own blood was applied to that Door. Our debt, laid upon Jesus and, with Him, nailed to the doorpost, the Cross, made public the Father's proclamation of forgiveness. Jesus said, "It is finished," thus, proclaiming to the world, the debt of mankind is, now, **"paid in full."**

Therefore, the Cross is the doorway to Heaven. Jesus, the Door, through which we must enter, makes possible the Way, for everyone. The debt, which would prevent our entering, was nailed there. Jesus, by His sacrifice, **took it out of the way.**

Jesus applied His own blood, to the debt laid upon him, and, then, decreed: **"It is finished,"** for evermore. By so doing, He was declaring its results will last and continue on, for eternity. Nothing of the past shall, ever, be brought up, against those entering.

When Noah and family stepped into the ark, Father God shut the door. I can hear a loud sound of **finality,** as the door swung shut and *a seal was set.* Their past, now, behind them, was locked out. That door fixed a great gulf between their *past,* that would be no more, and their *future,* that loomed on the horizon, on the other side.

38

COLOSSIANS 2:14

So, it is with our sin and past. God shut the door to it, on the cross. The devil cannot cross over it, to reach those *sealed by the blood*. And, the redeemed cannot cross that bloodline, to go back to what, once, was, but, now, is put under the blood. Those things no longer exist, but are removed, forever.

What Jesus accomplished on the cross, **perfects forever,** meaning nothing can be taken from it or anything added to it. What was done was **complete, perfect,** and **final,** never needing to be changed or modified. We need, only, to receive its perfect provision, for every need.

Jesus is the Door
I must enter,
into Eternal Life;

**Jesus is the sin
nailed to the Door,**
between hell and Heaven.

Jesus' blood on the Door
bought my Redemption,
and opened a Way
to **enter into Complete
and Perfect Salvation!**

Day 20

*For as in the days that were before the flood they were eating and drinking, marrying and giving in marriage, until the day Noah entered the ark, and knew not until the flood came, and **took them all away.***

Beware and Prepare!

Jesus is the **sin bearer.**[1] Either, He *bears our sin away*, or sin will *bear us away*, even, as the great floodwaters did the wicked.

"Your sin has **separated** you from your God," echoes in our ears, for sin, also, separates: First, from God; then, from each other; and, finally, the righteous from the unrighteous.[2]

Jesus, as the spiritual Ark, in whom Noah came to rest, would one day bear Noah's sin away. Therefore, the flood served, only, to *lift* him **higher** and **God ward.** The wicked, on the other hand, as God rejecters, were *buried beneath* its floodwaters of judgment. They were carried in an, entirely, different direction—to hell or perdition.

The righteous and the unrighteous were, thus, **separated.** As with Lazarus and the rich man, there was a *great gulf between*.[3] In this manner, the flood became the **great separator**, sending the two in different directions, to two different worlds and destinations.

Also, in the Day of the Son of Man, **an hour of separation** is coming, wherein the righteous and wicked will, again, be separated.[4] Their destinations will be that of opposite directions, in different realms.

God warns us to *watch* and *be ready*—so, that our families, or households, might not be **separated** from us.[5]

MATTHEW 24:38 & 39

But know this, that if the Goodman of the house had known in what watch the thief would come, he would have watched, and would not have suffered his house to be broken up.

Those, in Noah's day, did not *discern the time* and *the hour* of approaching judgment, until the flood came to **take them away**. If we do not **discern the hour** and prepare, our house could be *broken up*. Noah, a *faithful father,* **prepared** for his household. May we do the same!

Jesus my Sin-Bearer
carried my sin,
so into the Ark
I might step, right on in.

Noah built one
to house family
and carry them, safely,
over storm and rough sea.

What about me?

Day 21

Therefore, just as through one man sin entered the world, and death through sin, and thus death spread to all men, because all sinned.

A Curse Reversed

The **Jordan** meant *descending*.[1] Its waters emptied, or descended, into the Dead Sea. The Jordan River, descending from the city, **Adam,** ended in a place of **Death!**

The name **Adam** means *earthy* or ***taken out of the earth**.[2]* That which is *earthy* will proceed toward, or end in that, which is *death*!

The **descent of the Jordan** is a picture of that which occurred, because of Adam's sin. The sin of Adam *passed* or *flowed upon* all mankind.[3]

Ever since Adam's fall, the entire human race has been **descending** toward an **eternal death,** approaching their final plunge into its bottomless pit. Unless hindered, it will descend into **this place of no escape,** just, as the waters of the Jordan, flowing into the **Dead Sea,** *cannot flow out.*

There was, only, one thing that could *disrupt this continual flow* or *descent* of the River Jordan. God had to **intervene.** God had to **part its waters.**[4]

When God parted the waters of the Jordan, He **reversed its flow** clear back to Adam, and **cut off its flow** into the Dead Sea.[5] What a picture of the Salvation God has provided, through His **cleansing floods.**

Romans 5:12 NKJ

The **cleansing flow** of Jesus' blood **intervened** in our descent to the pit of death, *by washing* our past sins, **all the way back to Adam**. By so doing, God has **stopped our descending plunge** toward that final place of Death.

**Had not God intervened,
no hope of rescue
could be seen,**

for a race headed
straight for hell,
falling headlong, to a Sea
of Death, pell-mell.

**Sins' waters parted
in God's Son**
that at Adam had begun,

only, from there
to, continuously, swell,
until all mankind,
in its wake, too, fell.

Thank God!

The job has, now been, done.
**The waters have been parted
in God's Dear Son!**

Day 22

*Then goeth he, and taketh to him **seven other spirits more wicked** than himself; and they enter in, and dwell there: and **the last state of that man is worse that the first.***

PAYDAY!

Everything in the world has come upon this generation. That is because God is fixing to **repay** the devil.

Familiar spirits, of the past, have visited every evil, imaginable, upon this generation, **seven times worse,** while attempting to stop God's purpose from coming to pass and from its receiving what Jesus died to give it. But, **payday** is coming, as God's Remnant awaits the fullness of its inheritance and payment in full, of the Lord's Holy Spirit.

Jesus came to end cycles of generational curses, as He opens the door to generational blessings. **A most cursed generation can become one most blessed.**

As we position ourselves, to receive of His fullness, we become the Blessed. Curses of the past must be **reversed,** on our behalf and that of our seed that follows. The devil cannot prevent it.

Jesus stole the devil's keys and gave them to us. Now, we can open the windows of Heaven, to loose what is stored there, and bind the gates of hell, sending its foul contents back.

Then, we can **enter into the fullness** of what Jesus came to impart. We are the generation of the Remnant, upon whom the culmination of the generations must fall.

LUKE 11:26

Reach up to Heaven; call on His name; praise Him; bless Him; glorify Him. The work is done! We need, only, position our selves at the door, and, by faith, insert the key. **The buck stops here!**

Insert the key to be free
and inherit your Jubilee.

On bended knee, there agree:
every rich blessing to receive.

You have the faith, to seek His face,
given you through His saving Grace:

secured for thee, upon the tree:
dying to free, from the cursed seed.

His seed reigns,
eternal life to gain,
**from satan's pain
to reclaim.**

The buck stops here,
ending all fear.

**The curse, now, gone,
New Life does spawn.**

Day 23

*And of His **fullness** have all we **received**, and grace for grace.*

Fullness: At the Threshing Floor

The harvest is the *culmination* and *climax* of the entire year of labor: of plowing, sowing and watering the seed. After harvesting the grain, it is separated from the straw or chaff, **at the threshing floor.**

Ruth gleaned in the field of Boaz, where she was able to accumulate an ephah of barley, to share with her mother. But, later, **at the threshing floor,** betrothed to the harvest owner, Ruth left carrying 6 more ephahs of barley in her veil.

Notice, Ruth received **the fullness** of her *personal harvest,* when she came into *relationship* with Boaz, who is an Old Testament picture of Christ. Boaz, personally, placed this **treasure** in Ruth's veil. In other words, she left his presence, carrying *bread to feed* and *nourish the hungry,* wrapped in what, once, veiled her eyes from his.

In the New Testament, we witness a similar thing, as the disciples, toiling all night, caught nothing. At their Master's Word, they reentered the harvest, this time to **receive of His fullness.** They took up, so, many fish, that the **abundance broke their nets,** while threatening to sink their boat.

At that very moment, *His and their identities came into focus,* as they, distinctly, heard His call to follow Him and become fishers of men. If they would **embrace His vision,** they, too, would **share in His Harvest.**

When we go from **gleaning,** only, what we can, to **receiving** what the *Master wants to give,* the proportion of our harvest becomes

more than enough. What, once, would feed, just, a family, can, then, feed a city, a nation, or, a world. From Ruth's lineage, came the Messiah.

This happened to Joseph, as well. God, not only, gave him **enough grain** to feed his family and the nation of Egypt, but the budding nation of Israel and a waiting world.

God is desirous, that His Church come into Her **fullness,** so that He can **put treasure in Her sack,** as did Joseph, for his brothers. He wants to furnish Her limited view of Himself, with **bread enough,** for a waiting world.

It, may, mean **launching into the deep** at His Word, as the disciples, or **coming into His presence** and **waiting at His feet,** as Ruth. The result will be: **He gives increase.**

**Of Your fullness
have I desired,**

not, just, a servant
that's been hired,

receiving wages
that's been earned,

but **a fullness of
relationship have I yearned.**

Day 24

And the Angel of the LORD appeared to him in a flame of fire from the midst of a bush.

IN THE MIDST!

The waters have been rising and those in the Ark are being lifted. Like Noah, the Church is rising, in the **midst of the flood.**

Everything began in the mist. The Tree of Life was in the *midst of the Garden,* as was the Tree of the knowledge of good and evil. The issues of life proceed out of the *midst of our personal gardens,* within our hearts, where we must daily choose, from one of those two trees.

Adam ate fruit from the forbidden tree, in the *midst* of the Garden, plunging the entire human race into sin. God found His erring creation hiding, *amongst* the trees of the Garden, in fear of judgment. God's judgment fell, in the *midst* of great wickedness, in Noah's day, sweeping the wicked away in the *midst* of a great flood.

Difficulties, may, give rise to divine encounters, wherein Jesus walks to meet us, in the *midst* of great troubling situations. This happened with His disciples:

- The disciples sought Jesus in the *midst of their ship,* as fear gripped their hearts in the *midst of a raging storm.*

- Jesus came walking to His disciples in the *midst of the sea,* as they were toiling, in rowing.

Exodus 3:2 NKJ

Jesus will come to us, as well, in the *mist of our stormy sea*, whether consumed with fear, or toiling without results, to take us to the other side.

- **In the midst** of corruption and violence, Noah found favor and safe haven.

- **In the midst** of a heathenish, idolatrous people, Abraham's mind and name were changed!

- **In the midst** of an impossible situation, still gripping an impossible dream, Joseph rose to leadership, **in the midst** of a foreign land.

- **In the midst** of an ocean, **in the mist** of a fish's belly, Jonah's repentance led a city to repent.

As God's Church arises, **out of the midst of Her peril,** and like Elijah, calls down the fire of God, **in the midst of an unbelieving world,** then, not only a city, but a world can repent and be saved.

**I come to you
in the midst of your sea,**
to still the waves
and set you free.

I AM in your midst:
your Jubilee!

Day 25

*And He said, **Come**. And when Peter was come down out of the ship, he walked on the water, **to go to Jesus**.*

GOING TO THE OTHER SIDE

This *next move of God* is about **going to the other side**. The Remnant Church is **crossing over**.

After ordering His disciples to get in a boat and **go to the other side**, Jesus retreated, to be alone, in the Secret Place with His Father. Meanwhile, trouble arose, hindering progress toward reaching their goal.

Jesus came near His disciples, walking on the raging waves of the Sea, as they trembled with fear, in their distress. They saw Him walk on the very thing threatening them. Peter, inspired by His Master's example, found the courage to momentarily believe he, too, could **walk on the impossible**.

Today, overwhelming circumstances are wrecking havoc and destruction to many, out in their lifeboats, on threatening seas. Tossed to and fro, while trying to **cross to the other side,** they are in need of *someone* to show them the way, *anyone,* who is not afraid to **step out** of the *edge* of their boat, to do what they see their Master do.

By such example, if we, too, can, just, find the faith and courage to get out of our lifeboat and come to Jesus, when bidden, He will take our hand and give us the supernatural ability to **walk on top**. And, then, we will find we are walking on the **edge** of a miracle!

Matthew 14:29

Such miracles are "happening" at the **river's edge,** in this Third Day. As we step out, like Noah, His Grace will meet us and take us, where we've never been before, in God, and will cause us, there, to stand.

Grace much, more abounds. Therefore, Grace will *bear over every rough sea*, buoying upward, whereas sin lets down. Therefore, don't jump ship!

With Jesus aboard our ship of Grace, **we will reach the other side.** You will, either, sail the ship of sin, into death and hell, or the ship of Grace, onto the Crystal Sea.

Don't jump ship,
oh, child divine.

Abide in His Grace
and you will find,

the sailing gets smoother
the higher you climb,

on His wings of Grace
to those mansions sublime!

Day 26

*But when she could no longer hide him, she got a basket made of papy-rus reeds and waterproofed it with tar and pitch. She put the baby in the basket and laid it among the reeds along the **edge of the Nile River.***

At the River's Edge

Unusual things happened, **at the river's edge—**

- Joseph interpreted Pharaoh's dream, which took place at the **river's edge.**

- Moses was placed in an ark and, therein, hidden, at the **river's edge.**

- Elijah was caught up in a fiery chariot, leaving his mantle behind for Elisha, at the **river's edge.**

- Elisha, upon picking up Elijah's mantle, stepped into a new anointing, for a new ministry of double proportion, at the **river's edge.**

- Gideon's band of 300 were selected and called out, at the **river's edge.**

- Israel *crossed over* into the Promised Land, when in obedi-ence, Her priests, carrying the ark, stepped into the swollen Jordan, at the **river's edge.**

There has, always, had to be a priest, or *someone,* somewhere, willing to step into stormy surging waves or flooding rivers, in order to **open the way** for God's people, **to enter** into and inherit the prom-ises of God.

Exodus 2:3 NL

Breakthrough comes at the **river's edge!** It is at, just, such a place that God has, strategically, positioned His Church, to advance Her into the next move of God. There, He will propel Her through every attack, ever line of defense and strategy of the devil, into Her *future*, into the plan and purposes of God.

Miracles are "happening" at the **river's edge,** in this Third Day. As we step out, like Noah, to go where we've, never before, been in God, we will find—

In the **outcome,**
we have **overcome.**

The devil is **done,**
and we have **won!**

Meanwhile, is there *someone* willing to meet Jesus and walk on water? Is *anyone* willing to climb over the **edge** of the boat, and taking His hand, step out on the **edge of a miracle?**

**Step out of that boat
and into the River.**

Take the hand
of the mighty Deliverer!

Day 27

*For as in the days that were before the flood they were **eating and drinking, marrying and giving in marriage,** until the day that Noah entered the ark, and knew not until the flood came, and took them all away; so shall also the coming of the Son of man be.*

A Holy Ghost Party Don't Stop!

Like the wedding at Cana, if you want *a Holy Ghost party that doesn't stop*—**invite Jesus** to it![1]

The world is partying—only, **they have no wine!** They ran out, a long time ago. They served the best they had, first. They have not, yet, learned the importance of **including the wine-maker, Jesus,** to their list of guests, in their life's events. Therefore, they are *partying on,* not knowing their cups of joy are *empty!*[2]

The heathen of Noah's day had, long ago, **run out of the good stuff,** too. **There was no wine.** They had gone from wine to water, with not much sustenance or flavor, to pretty bland and bitter stuff! To, finally, **no water!** Nothing satisfied. How do I know? Everybody was busy hating, hurting and hitting one another, even, killing. They were angry about everything![3]

Our world has run out of wine and water, too. They are looking for the River, the Source, so they can *replenish their supply.* Only, when the servants of the LORD *do as Jesus says,* will the fount be found![4] God's servant Noah did, just, that and the rains came.

Noah went from being a **builder,** to being a **wine maker,** for his family in the new world, when he *obeyed* God.[5] The Israelites in Egypt went from **building** for the heathen, to being farmers and **carriers of wine,** in the New Land of Promise, when they *obeyed* God.

Matthew 24:38 & 39

The Church has been, busily, **building** for ages, too. Only, when She tires of building *after the fashion of this world,* and chooses to build, only, what God says build, *according to His pattern,* will She, finally, advance to being the **carrier of His New Wine!**

She must advance through the wildernesses, fires and floods, sent to develop, test and mature Her, in order to enter Her Promised Land, and come into the place She needs to be, in the Spirit, in order **to produce and carry this New Wine** to Her family and, then, to the world—that is, if She will **do whatever Jesus says** for Her to do![6]

Then, the **Holy Ghost party won't stop!** She won't get drunk, like Noah, but will be drunk on the *real thing![7]*

He'll turn **water into Wine**
filled with Joy, most divine,

if Jesus, as the guest,
is **invited, into our mess!**

Day 28

And the Angel of the Lord appeared to him in a flame of fire from the midst of a bush.

IN THE MIDST OF THE GARDEN

The waters have been rising and those in the Ark are being lifted. Like Noah, the Church is rising, in the **midst of the flood.**

Everything began in the midst. The Tree of Life was in the **midst of the Garden,** as was the Tree of the knowledge of good and evil.

Adam ate fruit from the forbidden tree, in the **midst of the Garden,** plunging the entire human race into sin. God found His erring creation, hiding **amongst the trees of the Garden,** in fear of judgment. They were hiding, in the very place, meant to **sanctuary** their daily encounter, with God.

The issues of life proceed, out of the **midst of our personal gardens,** within our hearts, where we must, daily, choose from one of those two trees.

Exodus 3:2 NKJ

A Watered Garden,
whose waters fail not.
A Garden watered,
by the Temple of God.

A Garden enclosed,
full of fruitful trees.
An enclosed Garden
with fragrance,
wafting the breeze.

A sound of Song,
rising in my ear.
It's the Song of Songs,
drawing me near:

To hear of His love
expressed for me,
the Love of Loves,
whose wine sets men free.

I will come and partake
of His Heavenly Cup.
I will come to this One
and, with gratitude, sup.

I will partake of wine
supplied for me,
from the fruit of the Vine,
crushed on Calvary's Tree.

This New Wine is
of such incredible degree.
Unlike the old,
its supply, eternally, free.

It comes from a Source
well supplied,
cleft out of the side
of He, who died.

Come to this Garden.
Come with me
and, there, partake
of this Crimson Tree.

It is a Tree of Life,
setting men free:

A Garden and a Tree,
supplied for you and for me.

Day 29

*Behold, I will send you Elijah the prophet before the coming of the dreadful day of the LORD: and **he shall turn the heart of the fathers to the children, and the heart of the children to their fathers,** lest I come and smite the earth with a curse.*

A Father's Heart

A father was **designed** to be the:

- **Provider**
- **Protector**
- **Priest**, and
- **Prophet** of his home.

Noah was all of these. We see Noah being **provider,** not, only, for his family, but the entire household on board the ark. At God's command, Noah filled the ark with amply food, for every creature aboard, for the five-month duration of the flood.[1]

Noah was **protector,** when he, "in holy fear built an ark, to save his family."[2]

As **priest,** Noah led his family in worshipful obedience to God, as they left the ark, following the flood, by building an altar, where he sacrificed animals and birds that had been approved for that purpose. "And the LORD was pleased with the sacrifice."[3]

As **prophet,** Noah talked with God. He heard and obeyed God's warning concerning the flood and built the ark, to the saving of his household.[4]

MALACHI 4:5 & 6 KJV

What else took place, in Noah's day, is also being repeated in ours, as fathers, again, fail to be the *provider, protector, priest,* and *prophet* of their homes. As a result, *protective services and various agencies,* in the place of the father, are trying to:

- minister clothing and physical **provision,** to destitute wives and children

- **protect** women and children, from those meant to be their *protector*

- rescue those, unwanted and uncared for, who due to a lack of a **priest/prophet** in the home, have grown up spiritually depraved.

Is it any wonder, that God's priority, in this end time, is that of restoring **father/child relationships?**

The Spirit of Elijah
has been sent,

by Father God,
whose heart's been rent,

by neglected children
and abandoned wives,

spent by messed up homes
and destroyed lives!

Day 30

And this is Eternal Life, that they may know You, the only True God, and Jesus Christ whom You have sent.

AWARENESS—A REALITY CHECK!

Father God, as our **Protector,** has given us Eternal Life. His abiding Presence, His Eternal Life, is a place of **security** and **safety**—for He "gives unto them Eternal Life and they shall **never perish.** "[1]

Eternal Life is an **awareness of God.** People thronged Jesus, day after day, seeking their needs to be met, eager to be taught, healed or fed. Jesus responded, gladly, to their eager anticipation.

But, somewhere in the crowd, *one* would come, who **sought Him.** One, who did not want *anything*, but, just, wanted to be **near the Great I Am.** One, who, just, longed to **experience more, of His Awesome Presence.**

To that longing heart, Jesus responded, most, graciously and gratefully. For, this one had caught the **Eternal Heart of God**—the longing of the heart to be **loved, for Oneself.**

While others sought material gain, teaching, or a message, this one, like Mary at Jesus' feet, wanted only, to be **near Him.** This longing brought comfort and a joyful satisfaction, to the loving heart of God. For, **Love longs to be received!**

To that one, God has given special promise—

> *Because he has* **set his love upon Me,** *therefore I will deliver him; I will set him on high, because he has* **known My name.** "[2]

JOHN 17:3 NKJ

Eternal Life is to **know** and be, ever, **conscious** of Him. It is a *new existence*, in which one is **aware of God,** in all that happens, in daily activity, every moment of life. Without this knowledge, one, just, **exists!**

God has not forgotten
His Awesome Plan,
wrapped up in
the Son of Man.

If I would **know**
this Father Dear,
to His Son
I must **draw near.**

When **upon Him**
I set my love,
He'll, then, lift me
to New Heights, Above,

Where He reveals
His Awesome Plan,
secrets revealed
to this New Man!

Day 31

Jesus Christ the same yesterday, and today, and forever.

LONGING FOR THE ETERNAL

There is a longing for the **eternal,** in all of us. Only the **Eternal One** can satisfy this **eternal longing.**

When people came to Jesus, seeking physical or emotional healing, all *legitimate needs,* Jesus, more than, gladly provided. However, more importantly, that most needed which lasts and cannot be done without, is not *temporal,* but **eternal.** This need, Jesus *longs,* most, to *fulfill.* This Jesus did, when He offered the woman at the well Living Water that **eternally** satisfies.

Above all, we must get this one need met, the *eternal longing* within that is satiable, only, by God, or all others, the *temporal,* will never satisfy. We continually search, going from need to need, miracle to miracle, healing to healing, even, supply to supply, yet, never finding the source, the spring or fountain, **from which all blessings flow.**

Once we find the *Source,* we can and will move from *one level to another.* This **eternal source** is the **Eternal God,** Himself. Therefore, it is **inexhaustible** and the boundaries **limitless.**

When we get plugged into this **main source,** we become a **channel** of His **incredible** and **inexhaustible** stream! Unlike the woman at the well, who came to a *natural* source to replenish her *exhaustible* supply, our supply will *never fail.* For, we draw from the Source, the Water of Life, *continuously flowing* from the eternally, inexhaustible Springs of God.

HEBREWS 13:8

There is a longing for the *fresh* and, *continuously, new* **Move of God** in every one of us. Man is searching for these **Eternal Springs**, issuing from the very, Throne of God, that can never be extinguished.

A longing for the Eternal
in our heart,
Father God, with purpose,
did impart.

A stamp of His image,
birthed from Above,
becomes a channel
of His awesome love.

One He must fill
to overflow,
**from His heart to our heart
an inexhaustible flow!**

Only, then, will we realize
how incredible this Source:

A stream of blessing, surpassing,
flowing from His heart,
through my heart
to yours!

His All Sufficiency

All I need came
through the Tree,
where Jesus died
to set me free.

By His Grace,
I shall receive
His all abounding
sufficiency.

For, through this access
shall I find,
all the riches
of His Glory, divine.

In no good thing,
shall I come behind.
For, in Christ Jesus,
all these riches are mine.

If by Grace,
I continue to abound,
in me, shall all
these riches be found.

For, by faith
I have full access,
into all He desired
that I possess.

And, I shall abundant
and fruitful be,
as I draw on the supply
of that eventful Tree.

For, out of that
barren, tree of death,
came a live Tree: His fullness
and likeness to possess.

A Tree that would bear
fruit, abundantly:
One that abounds,
in His all sufficiency!

NOTES

Day 1

1 See Hebrews 13:8.

Day 2

1 See Proverbs 23:7.
2 See 2 Corinthians 3:18.

Day 3

1 Romans 8:31–39

Day 4

1 See Numbers 14:2–3 and 16:13.

Day 7

1 See 1 Corinthians 2:9.
2 See 1 Corinthians 2:10.
3 See Revelations 4:1.
4 See 2 Corinthians 3:14–18.
5 See 1 John 4:17.
6 See Matthew 11:28.

Day 8

1 See Revelation 3:20.
2 See Genesis 7:1.
3 See Genesis 7:7.
4 See Genesis 7:4.
5 See Genesis 7:16.

Day 12

1 See Genesis 8:4.
2 See John 3:3–16.

Day 14

1 See John 19:30.
2 See 2 Timothy 1:12.
3 See Colossians 1:17 and Hebrews 1:3.

Day 16

1 Ed Vallowe, Biblical Mathematics, (Ed Vallowe Evangelistic Association, Georgia, 1988), p. 115.
2 Ibid, p. 108.
3 See Exodus 15:2
4 See Exodus 12:14–18
5 See I Corinthians 5:7

Day 17

1 See II Corinthians 6:16–17
2 See Romans 8:20

Day 18

1 Ed Vallowe, Biblical Mathematics, (Ed Vallowe Evangelistic Association, Georgia, 1988), p. 114–116.
2 Ibid.

Day 20

1 See 1 Peter 2:24.

2 See Isaiah 59:2.

3 See Luke 16:22-26.

4 See Matthew 25:34, 41.

5 See Matthew 24:43.

Day 21

1 Cornwall & Smith, *The Exhaustive Dictionary of Bible Names*, p. 155.

2 *Ibid*, p. 6.

3 See Romans 5:12.

4 See Joshua 3:13-17.

5 See Joshua 3:16.

Day27

1 See John 2:2.

2 See John 2:3.

3 See Genesis 6:11.

4 See John 2:5, 7-10.

5 Genesis 9:20-21.

6 See John 2:5.

7 See Ephesians 5:18.

Day29

1 See Genesis 6:21, 22.

2 See Hebrews 11:7.

3 See Genesis 8:20-21, LB.

4 See Hebrews 11:7.

Day 30

1 See John 3:16.

2 See Psalm 91:14.

ADDENDUM

If you have never made covenant with God and come into an intimate relationship with Him, you may do so, **RIGHT NOW!** It is much like taking the marriage vows, when you pledge your life to the one you love.

You, first, must admit that you have sinned. The Bible says your sins have separated you from God (Isaiah 59:1, 2). Therefore, to experience a relationship with God, your sins must be forgiven.

The Bible, further, explains that we are all born, spiritually, dead (Ephesians 2:1). Therefore, you need spiritual **LIFE**. The Bible calls this **Eternal Life** (John 10:28). It is the God-kind of Life, which never ends. It is, also, a quality kind of Life that is God's very own, full of joy, peace, and love (Galations 5:22-23).

To give us His Life, God had to send a substitute in our place to take the judgment for our sins; for the wages, or payment due sin, is **death** (Romans 6:23). God told Adam the day he sinned, he would, surely, die. That **death** *passed on* to Cain and on down through the generations, to every person, born into this world.

The **GOOD NEWS** is: Jesus was our substitute. He was the **PERFECT** Son of God, without sin. He was in Eternity with Father God, before the world began. Jesus was and is very God (John 1:1–3). He chose to become the baby in the manger, so He could have a body, with which to go to the cross for you and me (Hebrews 10:5).

The Bible, further, tells us, Jesus bore our sins and iniquities (Isaiah 53:4-5; 2 Corinthians 5:21). That means He not, only, paid the punishment for all the sins you, ever, committed, so you could be forgiven. But, He, also, took your sinful nature, or you, to the cross with Him, so you could be set free, from that within, which causes you to sin.

When one gets married, each gives up all rights to an independent life, agreeing to **SHARE LIFE** in a way that brings each, into agreement or **oneness** of relationship, in everything. All is done in **UNION**, with the one, to whom each pledges his or her life and love to—that is marriage! That is true covenant!

To experience this **ONENESS** in covenant with God, one must be willing to give up being independent, and the "me, me, me" attitude, of getting one's own way. If you are ready to surrender to God, in this way, making Him the center and the one in control of your life, to live your life in union with Him, pledging your love and desire, only, to Him, as a wife would her husband, then repeat a simple prayer, pledging your vows. But, like a true husband in love, God will not take advantage of your commitment to Him, by returning evil. The Bible says that what God has in mind for you is good, full of peace, blessing, and freedom, not evil (Jeremiah 29:11).

Pray:

God, I have sinned against You. I deserve death and separation from You. But, I believe You so loved me that You sent Jesus, to die for me. Because of the death He died and the blood He shed, I can be forgiven and set free from sin and who I was, while in rebellion against You. Right now, I receive Jesus as my Savior and Lord. Much like a marriage on earth, I pledge You my love and obedience. I surrender my will to You, realizing my life is no longer mine.

*In return, I receive forgiveness for my sins (past, present, and future). I receive Eternal Life. And, I come into covenant relationship with You, meaning we will, now, walk in intimate fellowship. I do not, fully, understand all about this, but I know, as I come to know You, intimately, I will grow and will become one with You, more every day. Therefore, I will spend time, **ALONE, WITH YOU**—talking to You in prayer, listening to You, hearing Your voice in Your Word (the Bible), so I might know what You want me to do and be like, seeking to please, only, You. I pledge my love to You, alone, meaning I will cleave to You and not to the world, its attractions and, even, close friends. Here is my heart, take it and make it Your own and Your home. Thank You for giving Yourself for me and to me, that I might live with You, forever. AMEN!*

Having prayed this prayer, you have, just, entered into an eternal contract, or covenant of promise, with God. Be aware of this—you, now, have an enemy, even, more committed to your destruction. Like an old "flame" or close friend, with whom you have "gone out," he will try to persuade you to return. He does not give up, easily. How successful you are in walking, victoriously, in this new life and intimate relationship with God, will be determined by how much you love Him, how *completely* you submit your will and desires to Him, and how *devotedly* you seek and cleave, only, to Him.

Just, as there are witnesses, when you get married, so this marriage contract needs witnesses. Romans 10:9 says we are to **CONFESS** with our mouth, Jesus, as our Lord. In other words, **TELL SOMEBODY** your decision. Jesus promised that, if we confess Him **BEFORE MEN,** He will confess us **BEFORE HIS FATHER,** in Heaven.

Next, determine to be *faithful* to the Lord and His church. Hebrews 10:25 emphasizes the importance of this, in the days, in which we are living: "Let us *not neglect* our church meetings, as some people do, but encourage and *warn* each other, especially, now that the day of His coming back, again, is drawing near" (LB). Therefore, the most important thing you can do, along with those things, already, mentioned, is find the church where God would have you attend and be faithful. This will be your **own, spiritual family**, where you are fed, nurtured and cared for, as you grow. You cannot be strong, or victorious, without it. Do it, today!

God bless you.

www.ingramcontent.com/pod-product-compliance
Lightning Source LLC
Chambersburg PA
CBHW060038050426
42448CB00012B/3062